A TRUE BOOK™

WITHDRAWN

Planet Neptune

ANN O. SQUIRE

Children's Press®
An Imprint of Scholastic Inc.
New York Toronto London Auckland Sydney
Mexico City New Delhi Hong Kong
Danbury, Connecticut

Content Consultant

Bryan C. Dunne

Assistant Chair, Assistant Professor, Department of Astronomy

University of Illinois at Urbana–Champaign

Urbana, Illinois

Library of Congress Cataloging-in-Publication Data
Squire, Ann.
 Planet Neptune / by Ann O. Squire.
   pages cm. — (A true book)
 Includes bibliographical references and index.
 ISBN 978-0-531-21155-7 (lib. bdg.) — ISBN 978-0-531-25361-8 (pbk.)
 1. Neptune (Planet)—Juvenile literature. I. Title.
 QB691.S65 2014
 523.48—dc23   2013026059

All rights reserved. Published in 2014 by Children's Press, an imprint of Scholastic Inc.
Printed in China 62
SCHOLASTIC, CHILDREN'S PRESS, A TRUE BOOK™, and associated logos are trademarks and/or registered trademarks of Scholastic Inc.

1 2 3 4 5 6 7 8 9 10 R 23 22 21 20 19 18 17 16 15 14

Front cover: The *Voyager 2* spacecraft as it passes by Neptune

Back cover: The *Voyager 2* spacecraft

Find the Truth!

Everything you are about to read is true *except* for one of the sentences on this page.

Which one is **TRUE**?

T or F   Neptune has the longest year of any planet in our solar system.

T or F   Huge oceans of water on Neptune's surface cause the planet's blue color.

Find the answers in this book.

Contents

THE BIG TRUTH!

Neptune is much larger than Earth.

Voyager 2 became the longest operating spacecraft in August 2012.

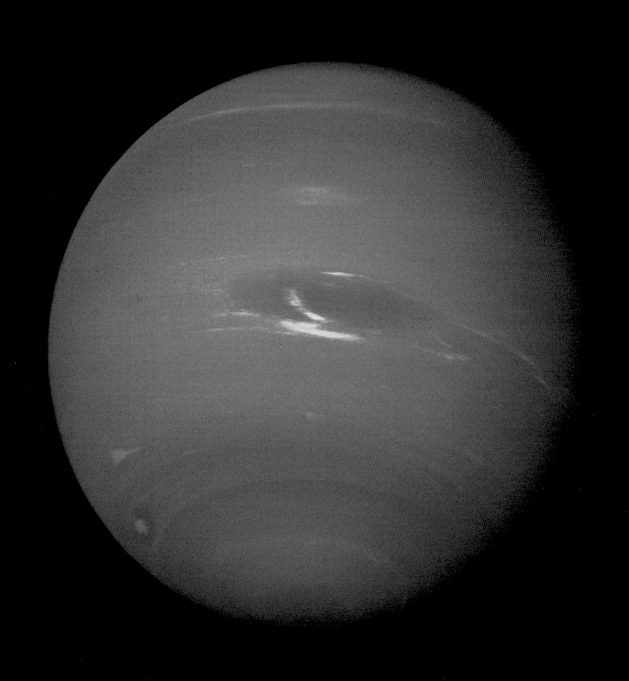

CHAPTER 1

The Blue Planet

Far out into space, farther than the naked eye can see, lies a cold, blue world. It is the **planet** Neptune. Neptune is an average of 2.8 billion miles (4.5 billion kilometers) from the sun. That is 30 times farther from the sun than Earth is. It is no surprise that Neptune is the coldest and darkest planet in our solar system.

The *Voyager 2* spacecraft took this photo 4.4 million miles (7.1 million km) from Neptune.

The Farthest Planet

Neptune is one of the eight planets that **orbit** the sun. It is the farthest planet from the sun. It is also the third largest of all the planets. Only the gas giants Jupiter and Saturn are more massive. Along with Jupiter, Saturn, and Uranus, Neptune is one of the outer planets. They are the most distant planets from the sun. The inner planets are Mercury, Venus, Earth, and Mars.

The inner planets have solid surfaces. Neptune and the other outer planets do not.

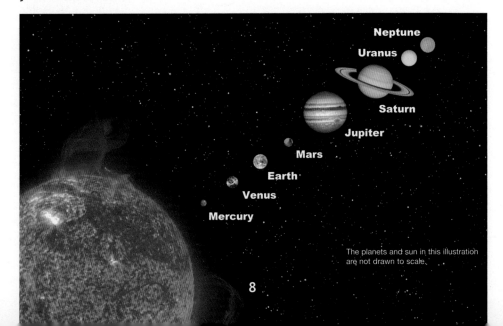

Neptune

Uranus

Saturn

Jupiter

Mars

Earth

Venus

Mercury

The planets and sun in this illustration are not drawn to scale.

 It takes light more than four hours to travel from the sun to Neptune.

Distance From the Sun

All planets have slightly **elliptical** orbits. However, Neptune's orbit is almost circular. Its farthest point from the sun is called the aphelion. Neptune's aphelion is more than 2.82 billion miles (4.54 billion km) away. Its closest point is called the perihelion. It is more than 2.77 billion miles (4.46 billion km) away. Considering these huge distances, the difference between the aphelion and perihelion is not very much.

Even at its closest point to Earth, Neptune cannot be seen with the naked eye from our planet.

Distance From Earth

Neptune and Earth are always moving through space. As a result, the distance between them constantly changes. They are closest when they are on the same side of the sun. Then they can be as close as 2.7 billion miles (4.3 billion km) apart. The distance increases when their orbits place them on opposite sides of the sun. Then it is closer to 2.9 billion miles (4.7 billion km).

A Big Planet

Neptune is one of the largest planets in our solar system. It measures more than 30,000 miles (48,000 km) across. This is almost four times as wide as Earth. It would take more than 57 Earth-size objects to fill the space occupied by Neptune. Neptune also has 17 times the **mass** of Earth.

This illustration shows how Earth's size compares to Neptune's size.

Spinning Planet

Like all planets in our solar system, Neptune rotates on its **axis**. On Earth, one rotation takes about 24 hours. On Neptune, the average rotation time is much shorter: just more than 16 hours. But here is something strange. Different parts of Neptune rotate at different speeds. At the **equator**, one full rotation takes 18 hours. At the poles, it only takes about 12 hours!

On average, the sun rises about every 16 hours on Neptune.

High winds carry clouds in streaks across Neptune's atmosphere. Scientists have measured Neptune cloud streaks as long as 124 miles (200 km).

Why do different parts of the planet rotate at different speeds? It is because Neptune is made up of gases and liquids. Earth's liquid outer **core** also rotates at a different speed than its more solid layers. However, the difference in speeds is much less than on Neptune. The differences in rotation speed on Neptune help create driving winds. In fact, the planet experiences some of the strongest winds in the solar system.

The sun appears smaller from Neptune than it does from Earth.

A Year on Neptune

Because Neptune is the farthest planet from the sun, its orbit is larger than that of any other planet. Neptune must travel more than 17 billion miles (27 billion km) to go just once around the sun. As you might imagine, this takes a long time. A year is the time it takes a planet to make one orbit around the sun. One year on Neptune is equal to almost 165 Earth years!

A Recent Discovery

Depending on how you look at it, it was not all that long ago that Neptune was discovered. In Earth years, about 170 years have passed since **astronomers** first spotted the planet through a telescope. But Neptune has completed only one trip around the sun in that time. This means that in Neptunian years, a little more than one year has gone by since its discovery.

Astronomers first saw Neptune through the telescope at the Berlin Observatory in Germany in 1846.

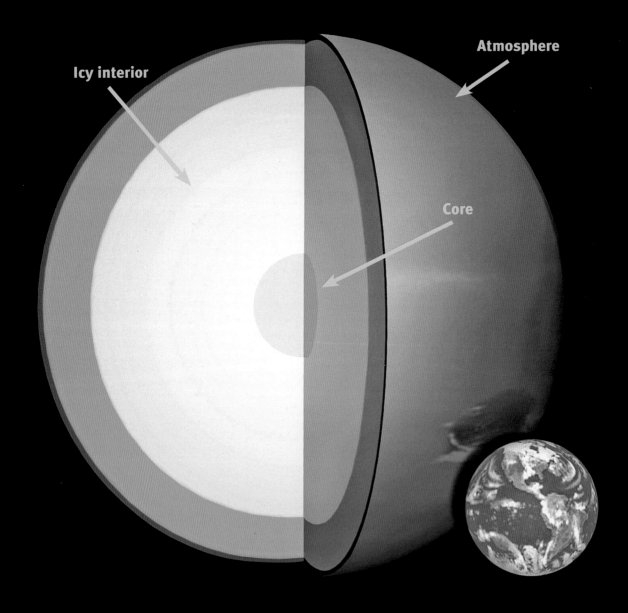

Icy interior

Atmosphere

Core

CHAPTER 2

A World of Liquid and Gas

Like the other outer planets, Neptune has a thick outer **atmosphere**. It is made up of hydrogen, helium, and small amounts of methane. Nearer the planet's interior, the pressure increases. The gases give way to an interior of water, ammonia, and methane. These substances are known as ices, so scientists refer to this layer as "icy." But it is actually very hot! The center of Neptune is a solid rock and metal core.

 Neptune's core is about the size of Earth.

From Cold to Hot

The gases at the tops of the clouds in Neptune's atmosphere are very cold. The average temperature of this layer is −346 degrees Fahrenheit (−210 degrees Celsius). Closer to the planet's center, temperatures are higher. The liquid inner layer is much hotter than the outer gas layer. The liquid can reach more than 3,000°F (1,649°C). The rocky core is the hottest of all. Temperatures there can reach 9,260°F (5,127°C).

Far from the sun's warmth, Neptune's exterior is extremely cold.

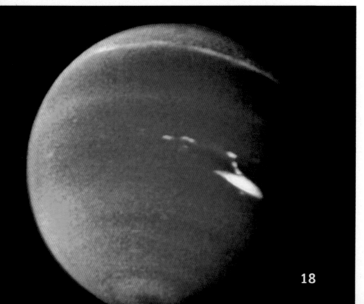

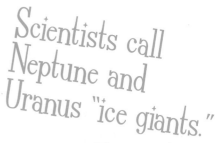

Scientists call Neptune and Uranus "ice giants."

Methane is the primary element in natural gas, which fuels many stoves.

Methane Blue

Neptune's beautiful blue color is caused by methane. This is one of the gases that make up the planet's atmosphere. Methane absorbs light from the red end of the color spectrum. It does not absorb blue light. Instead it reflects it back, so the planet appears blue.

Ammonia, which gives Jupiter its color, is sometimes used in cleaning products.

Gases in the Atmosphere

The color of a gas planet can tell us some details about its atmosphere. All the giant planets have atmospheres primarily of hydrogen and helium. But they have small amounts of other elements, too. The planet Uranus is like Neptune in many ways. For example, Uranus also appears blue. Not surprisingly, its atmosphere contains small amounts of methane. Jupiter and Saturn get their orange and yellow colors from ammonia gases in their atmospheres.

High Winds

Neptune has some of the most violent weather of any planet in our solar system. Wind speeds can reach more than 1,300 miles per hour (2,092 kph). That is three times faster than winds recorded on Jupiter. It is nine times faster than the strongest hurricane winds here on Earth.

Neptune's winds whip clouds around the planet. Sometimes, huge storms are created, such as the large spot in the bottom left of this photo.

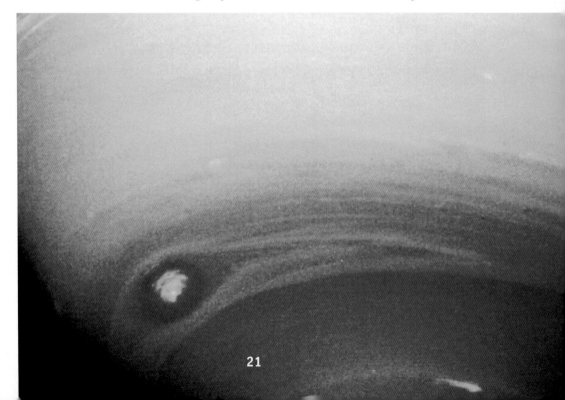

Powerful Storms

Like Jupiter and Saturn, Neptune has giant storms that circle the planet. In 1989, the *Voyager 2* spacecraft spotted a huge storm on Neptune. Scientists at the National Aeronautics and Space Administration (NASA) called the storm the Great Dark Spot. It measured 8,100 miles (13,036 km) across. That is three times wider than the United States!

Bright, white smudges of clouds followed Neptune's Great Dark Spot.

22

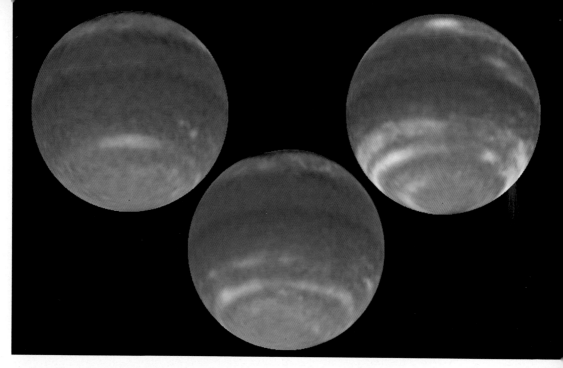

Hubble's photographs of Neptune showed new storms, but the Great Dark Spot had gone.

Changing Weather

Weather on Neptune seems to change much faster than it does on other planets. The Hubble Space Telescope sent back images of Neptune a few years after the Great Dark Spot was first photographed. The huge storm was nowhere to be seen! In contrast, Jupiter's storm called the Great Red Spot has been raging for more than 400 years.

CHAPTER 3

Discovering Neptune

Some planets are bright enough or close enough to Earth that we can easily see them shining in the night sky. Mars, Venus, and Jupiter are all examples. These planets have been known since ancient times. Neptune, on the other hand, is so far away that it can only be seen through a telescope. Telescopes powerful enough to see Neptune have existed for just a few hundred years.

The best time to spot Neptune is from July to November.

A Mathematical Discovery

Unlike the way most planets were discovered, Neptune was not discovered by an astronomer peering through a telescope. It was the strange behavior of a different planet that led to Neptune's discovery. In the early 1800s, scientists were studying the planet Uranus. They had calculated where it would appear in the sky on a certain day based on its orbit. But Uranus did not appear exactly where the scientists had predicted.

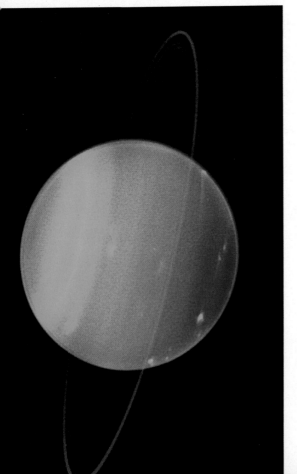

Scientists were studying Uranus when aspects of its orbit indicated the presence of another nearby planet.

26

Urbain Le Verrier predicted an asteroid belt between Mercury and the sun. Today we know it does not exist.

They were unable to explain the finding. Some scientists decided that the gravity of another, unseen planet must be influencing the orbit of Uranus. French mathematician Urbain Le Verrier calculated the location of this mystery planet. But he had a difficult time convincing astronomers to take his prediction seriously.

Johann Gottfried Galle was the assistant director of the Berlin Observatory in Germany when he first saw Neptune.

Neptune Through a Telescope

In 1846, a German astronomer named Johann Gottfried Galle tested Le Verrier's prediction. Using Le Verrier's calculations, Galle pointed his telescope toward the sky. There was Neptune! It was almost exactly where Le Verrier had predicted it would be.

Naming Neptune

Scientists and the public were amazed that a planet could be discovered using math. For a while, the new planet was known as Le Verrier's Planet. It was Le Verrier himself who suggested the name Neptune. This was the name of the Roman god of the sea. What better name for a blue planet than that of a god of oceans?

The god Neptune can be identified by his trident, or three-pronged spear.

A Most Unusual Moon

Neptune's largest moon is Triton. It is one of the strangest places in our solar system. Its surface is wrinkled and pitted like the skin of a cantaloupe. A shiny crust of frozen nitrogen covers its surface. Triton is also the coldest known object in the solar system. Its average surface temperature is −400°F (−240°C).

Unlike most moons, Triton is geologically active. "Ice volcanoes" spew plumes of frozen material high into Triton's sky. Strong winds blow the material in streaks across the moon.

Triton also orbits backward. That is, it orbits in the direction opposite Neptune's rotation. It is the only large moon in the solar system that orbits this way.

Neptune's gravity pulls on Triton. This slows the moon down and draws it closer to the planet. In billions of years, Triton will either crash into Neptune or be torn apart by the planet's gravity.

A crescent Triton (bottom) appears below Neptune in this photo taken by the *Voyager 2* spacecraft.

CHAPTER 4

Neptune's Moons and Rings

Neptune has both moons and rings, although they are not as spectacular as Saturn's. Fourteen moons had been discovered by 2013. Triton is the largest. It is about three-fourths the size of Earth's moon. Neptune's smallest moon was found in July 2013. It measures just 12 miles (19 km) from one side to the other. This moon is only 16,400 miles (26,393 km) from Neptune. Scientists estimate that it orbits the planet in only 23 hours.

Triton and Nereid

Triton was the first of Neptune's moons to be discovered. Astronomers spotted it in 1846, just 17 days after Neptune itself was first identified. William Lassell, an English merchant, made the discovery. More than 100 years passed before a second Neptunian moon was discovered. Astronomer Gerald Kuiper spotted Nereid through a huge, ground-based telescope. Nereid is a small moon, measuring only 110 miles (177 km) across.

William Lassell also discovered two of Uranus's moons: Ariel and Umbriel.

William Lassell stands at his telescope.

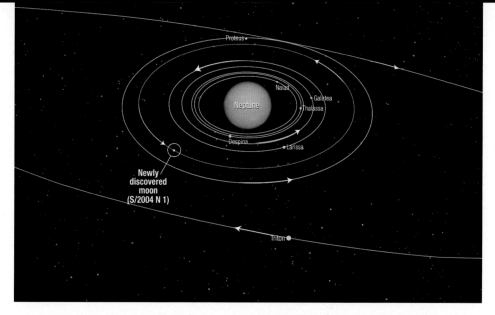

The moon discovered in 2013 was originally called S/2004 N1.

More Moons

After Nereid, no moons were spotted until 1989. That year, *Voyager 2* revealed six more moons orbiting Neptune. Five more were seen in 2002 and 2003 through ground-based telescopes. The Earth-orbiting Hubble Space Telescope discovered another in 2013. Neptune's moons include Triton, Nereid, Despina, and Proteus. Neptune is the god of the sea. Its moons are named after mythical beings associated with oceans or the god Neptune.

Dark Rings

Neptune has rings, but they are difficult to see from Earth. Astronomers long suspected that rings might exist, but they did not have proof. Finally, *Voyager 2* sent back photos of them during its 1989 mission. The rings are made up of dust and small pieces of debris. Scientists think they might have formed when one of Neptune's moons was destroyed.

Timeline of Neptune Discoveries

1989

Voyager 2 flies past Neptune, becoming the first and only spacecraft to visit the planet.

1846

Urbain Le Verrier calculates Neptune's location, allowing Johann Gottfried Galle to spot the planet through a telescope. William Lassell discovers the moon Triton soon after.

Why are Neptune's rings so dark while Saturn's are so shiny and bright? Saturn's rings contain mostly ice. Have you ever been outside on a sunny winter day? Then you probably noticed that ice reflects a lot of the sun's light. Neptune's rings contain more rocks and dust. These do not reflect as much light. This makes the rings darker and more difficult to see.

2003
Astronomers discover five more moons orbiting Neptune.

2013
Hubble photographs reveal a 14th moon orbiting Neptune.

CHAPTER 5

Exploring Neptune and Beyond

Neptune has not been explored as much as planets closer to Earth have been. In fact, the only spacecraft to visit is *Voyager 2*. Two *Voyager* spacecraft were launched in 1977. After passing by Jupiter and Saturn, *Voyager 1* continued out beyond the solar system. *Voyager 2* also flew past Jupiter and Saturn, as well as Uranus. Then it traveled on to Neptune.

Voyager 2 (left) was launched first, in August 1977. Voyager 1 was launched in September.

Important Mission

Voyager 2 flew by Neptune 12 years and 4.4 billion miles (7 billion km) after its launch. It came within about 3,000 miles (4,830 km) of the planet. It was also able to take a closer look at the moon Triton as it passed by. Almost everything we know about Neptune came from the *Voyager* mission. The spacecraft discovered moons, rings, and stormy weather. *Voyager 2* also took the only close-up photos of the planet.

Voyager 2 **took photos of Neptune and its moons over the course of several days.**

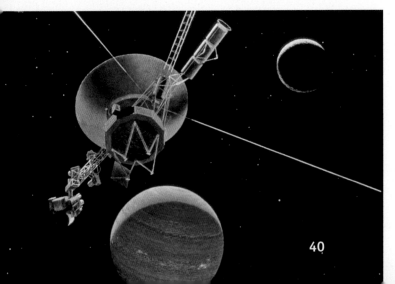

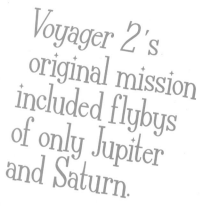

Voyager 2's original mission included flybys of only Jupiter and Saturn.

40

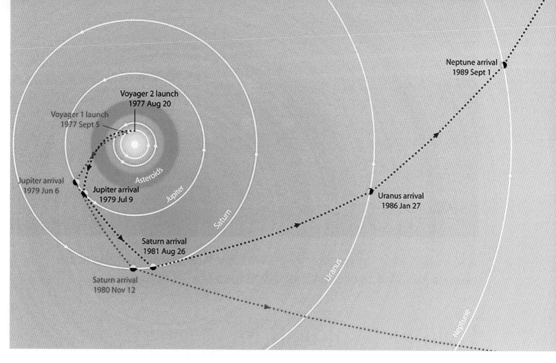

Voyager 2 launch
1977 Aug 20

Voyager 1 launch
1977 Sept 5

Neptune arrival
1989 Sept 1

Jupiter arrival
1979 Jun 6

Jupiter arrival
1979 Jul 9

Asteroids

Jupiter

Saturn

Uranus arrival
1986 Jan 27

Saturn arrival
1981 Aug 26

Saturn arrival
1980 Nov 12

Uranus

Neptune

This illustration shows the paths of both *Voyager* spacecraft through and beyond the solar system.

Out of the Solar System

After flying by Neptune, *Voyager 2* kept going. It charted a course that will eventually take it out of our solar system. As they travel, both *Voyager 1* and *2* continue to send data back to scientists on Earth. Both spacecraft carry a plaque with images of life on Earth. This is in case the spacecraft are ever found by intelligent life-forms.

The Very Large Telescope can combine the power of four main telescopes and four smaller, additional telescopes.

Further Exploration

Studies of Neptune did not end with *Voyager 2*. The *New Horizons* spacecraft took photos of Neptune and Triton as it made its way toward Pluto. The Very Large Telescope in Chile and other ground-based observatories are also looking at Neptune. Orbiting telescopes are watching, too. New discoveries are always being made, from new moons to a warm south pole. With so many questions left to answer about Neptune, who knows what scientists will find next?

The Hubble Space Telescope

Launched in 1990, the Hubble Space Telescope orbits Earth once every 97 minutes. Above Earth's atmosphere, Hubble has a much better view than ground-based telescopes have. It has sent back hundreds of thousands of photos of our solar system, including images of Neptune. The Hubble Space Telescope is currently one of our best ways to learn about the blue planet. In fact, astronomers first spotted Neptune's 14th moon in 2013 with the help of Hubble photographs!

True Statistics

Speed at which Neptune orbits the sun: 12,150 mph (19,554 kph)

Number of years it would take to reach Neptune when traveling at 75 mph (121 kph): 4,110

Number of Neptunian days in a Neptunian year: 60,190

Number of moons orbiting Neptune: At least 14

Distance between Neptune and *Voyager 2* as the spacecraft flew by in 1989: 2,983 mi. (4,801 km)

Length of each season on Neptune: A little more than 41 Earth years

Did you find the truth?

(T) Neptune has the longest year of any planet in our solar system.

(F) Huge oceans of water on Neptune's surface cause the planet's blue color.

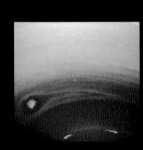

Resources

Books

Aguilar, David A. *13 Planets: The Latest View of the Solar System*. Washington, DC: National Geographic, 2011.

Meekins, Jeannie. *14 Fun Facts About Neptune: A 15-Minute Book*. LearningIsland.com, 2011.

Visit this Scholastic Web site for more information on Neptune:
★ www.factsfornow.scholastic.com
Enter the keyword **Neptune**

Important Words

astronomers (uh-STRAH-nuh-muhrz) — scientists who study stars, planets, and space

atmosphere (AT-muhs-feer) — the mixture of gases that surrounds a planet

axis (AK-sis) — an imaginary line through the middle of an object, around which that object spins

core (KOR) — the most inner part of a planet

elliptical (i-LIP-tih-kuhl) — in a flat oval shape

equator (i-KWAY-tur) — an imaginary line around the middle of a planet or other body that is an equal distance from the north and south poles

mass (MAS) — the amount of physical matter that an object contains

orbit (OR-bit) — to travel in a path around something, especially a planet or the sun

planet (PLAN-it) — a large body orbiting a star

Index

Page numbers in **bold** indicate illustrations

About the Author

Ann O. Squire is a psychologist and an animal behaviorist. Before becoming a writer, she studied the behaviors of rats, tropical fish in the Caribbean, and electric fish from central Africa. Her favorite part of being a writer is the chance to learn as much as she can about all sorts of topics. In addition to *Mars*, *Jupiter*, *Mercury*, *Neptune*, and *Saturn*, Squire has written about many different animals, from lemmings to leopards and cicadas to cheetahs. She lives in Long Island City, New York.